Power Racers

Shoo Rayner ✳ **Jonatronix**

OXFORD
UNIVERSITY PRESS

Chapter 1 – The dusty box

Tiger and his dad were in the garage.

"Come and help me, Tiger!" said Dad.
"This rotten old box is falling apart!"

As Tiger and his dad lifted the box on to the
workbench, they knocked over some bits
of drainpipe.

"Put those on the workbench,
too," said Dad.

"Hi, Tiger. What's going on?" It was Ant. Max and Cat were with him.

Tiger smiled. He was pleased to see his friends. "We're clearing out the garage," he explained.

Dad blew the dust off the old box. "This is something I think you kids might like," he said.

Max helped Tiger take the lid off the box.

"Wow! Electric racing cars!" said Tiger. "Can we play with them?"

"Of course," said Tiger's dad. "You can set up the track in here while I take this rubbish to the dump. Don't drive too fast!"

The four friends put the racing track pieces together. Ant switched on the power.

"I'm having the blue car!" said Max.

"I'll racc you," said Tiger, who was holding the red car.

The boys fitted their cars into the metal slots on the track.

Tiger gave Max a hand controller and showed him how it worked. "You press the trigger like this ..."

The cars zoomed round the track!

"This is fun!" Max yelled. He skilfully drove his car around the sharp corners of the track.

Meanwhile, Cat and Ant were looking at the other cars.

"What are you doing?" Cat asked.

Ant was measuring a green car with his fingers.

"If we were small," he said, "we could fit inside these cars. Then we could drive them!"

Cat peeped inside the yellow car.

"There are no seat belts," she said.

Ant held up some rubber bands. "Oh, yes there are!"

Then Ant pulled the helmets off two model soldiers that had been in the box. "We can use these as crash helmets."

Cat turned the dial on her watch and …

She fastened her seat belt and put on a crash helmet.

Ant picked up a controller.

"Be careful with that!" exclaimed Cat.

Suddenly, there was a *BANG!*

Max and Tiger's cars had spun off the track. Max had tried to overtake Tiger's car on the corner. Both cars were going too fast. They smashed into each other and skidded across the garage floor.

"That was great!" Max cheered.

"Let's try again," said Tiger.

As Tiger bent down to pick up his car, he saw Cat in the yellow car.

"Hey, what are you doing in there?" Tiger said. "Girls can't drive!"

"We'll see about that," Cat shouted back.

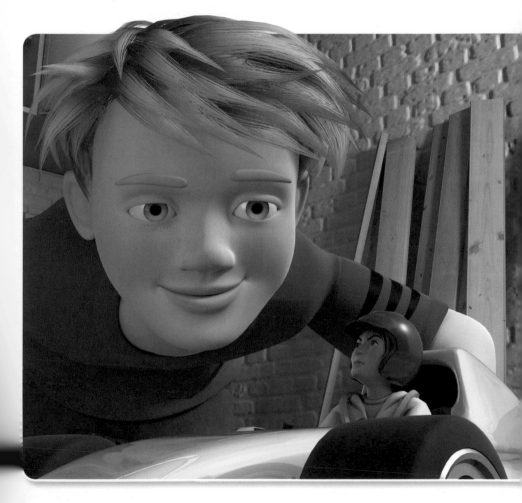

Tiger turned the dial on his watch. He put on a helmet and strapped himself inside the red car.

"Max, you control my car!" Tiger shouted.

"But I need to keep a lookout, in case your dad comes back," warned Max.

"I need your help!" Tiger yelled back. "We'll hear Dad when he comes home."

Max wasn't so sure, but he picked up the controller anyway.

Cat and Tiger revved their engines.

Max loomed above them. "Are you ready?" his voice boomed.

Cat and Tiger nodded.

"GO!" yelled Ant.

The two cars sped down the track. Cat was in the lead. She couldn't see Tiger.

"There are no mirrors," Cat said to herself.

She flipped up her watch. Four coloured dots appeared on the screen. The red dot told her that Tiger was right behind her. He was catching up fast.

Cat's watch beeped an alarm. Tiger's car screeched and crashed into hers.

The engines roared as the two cars left the track and sped across the floor.

Max and Ant jabbed the buttons on their controllers. They couldn't bring Cat and Tiger's cars back on to the track.

"The cars are out of control!" Ant yelled.

"There aren't any brakes!" Tiger called back.

Tiger's front wheel bumped into some planks of wood stacked against the wall.

"Look out!" Max's voice boomed above them.

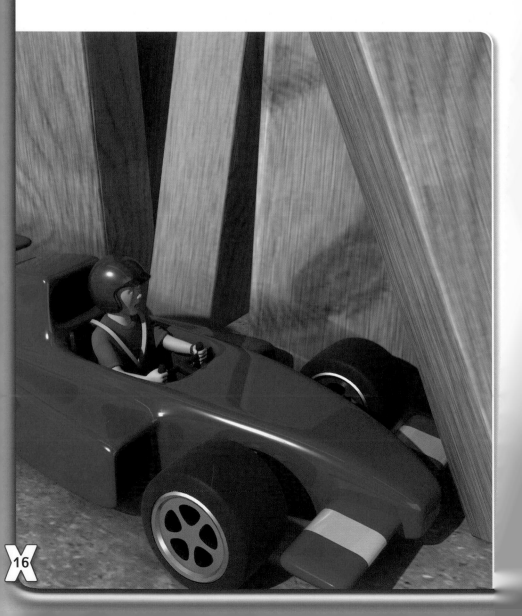

Chapter 5 – Off the track

The two drivers weaved in and out, as the planks crashed down around them.

Tiger steered his car up a piece of plastic gutter that was leaning against a shelf.

Cat was behind him now.

As the cars sped along the shelf, the paint pots wobbled and crashed down behind them.

There was paint everywhere!

The cars zoomed off the end of the shelf. They flew through the air and landed on the workbench.

"Tunnels ahead!" Tiger yelped.

Cat and Tiger shot in and out of the bendy drainpipe tunnels.

"Arrgghhh!" Tiger screamed.

It was pitch dark.

"Oh, no!" Cat's voice echoed along the dark tube. "This pipe is in the cardboard box. We will crash into the bottom of the box!"

Max and Ant held their breath.
There was nothing they could do.

R-R-R-R-IP! A hole appeared in the
bottom of the cardboard box. The cars burst
through the hole. They flew through the air
above the hard, concrete garage floor.

Max and Ant dived to catch them but
missed. The cars bounced off Tiger's old
space hopper. Both cars flipped in the air and
bounced again on Tiger's football.

Cat and Tiger's engines spluttered
and stopped.

There was silence for a moment.

The cars landed on one of the planks of wood they had knocked over earlier.

Like a seesaw, the plank sank under their weight. It dropped down and the cars rolled back on to the tracks. They locked back in place.

The finishing line was only half a metre away.

Max and Ant pushed the buttons on their controllers. Cat and Tiger's cars sped across the finishing line together.

"That was brilliant!" said Max.

"So, girls can't drive, hey?" said Cat, pulling off her helmet.

"Sorry," said Tiger, sheepishly.

Suddenly, they heard a *real* car.

"Uh, oh," said Max.

Cat and Tiger quickly turned the dials on their watches and were instantly back to their normal size.

Tiger's dad came into the garage. "So, who won the race?" he asked.

"Um … it was a draw!" said Tiger, winking to Cat.